Pebble® Plus

Physical Science

All Kinds of Motion

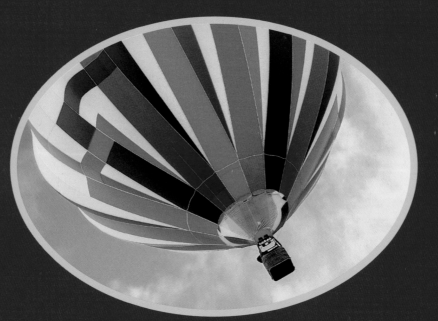

by Jennifer Waters

CAPSTONE PRESS
a capstone imprint

Pebble Plus is published by Capstone Press,
151 Good Counsel Drive, P.O. Box 669, Mankato, Minnesota 56002.
www.capstonepub.com

Books published by Capstone Press are manufactured with paper
containing at least 10 percent post-consumer waste.

Library of Congress Cataloging-in-Publication Data
Waters, Jennifer.
 All kinds of motion / by Jennifer Waters
    p. cm.—(Pebble Plus. Physical science)
 Includes bibliographical references and index.
 ISBN 978-1-4296-6607-7 (library binding)
 1. Motion—Juvenile literature. 2. Kinematics—Juvenile literature.
I. Title.
 QC133.5.W369 2011
 531'.11—dc22   2010034309

Summary: Simple text and color photographs introduce kinds of motion, including motion powered by wind, water, and
electricity.

Editorial Credits
Gillia Olson, editor; Veronica Correia, designer; Eric Gohl, media researcher; Laura Manthe, production specialist

Photo Credits
Capstone Studio/Karon Dubke, cover, 20–21 (all)
Shutterstock/Carsten Reisinger, 11; Chaikovskiy Igor, 5; Denis Tabler, 7; dwphotos, 19; Ramona Heim, 9; Tito Wong, 17;
    wiw, 13; Xin Qiu, 1; Yuriy Kulyk, 15

Note to Parents and Teachers

The Physical Science series supports national standards related to physical science. This
book describes and illustrates motion. The images support early readers in understanding
the text. The repetition of words and phrases helps early readers learn new words. This book
also introduces early readers to subject-specific vocabulary words, which are defined in the
Glossary section. Early readers may need assistance to read some words and to use the Table of
Contents, Glossary, Read More, Internet Sites, and Index sections of the book.

Printed in the United States of America in North Mankato, Minnesota.
092010
005933CGS11

Table of Contents

Motion All Around

Every day you travel

more than a million miles.

You're on planet Earth,

traveling around the sun.

The Earth moves through space.

Earth also spins once each day,

which causes day and night.

We can't feel the Earth move,

but it affects us every day.

Motion is all around us.

Wind

Wind is moving air. Sunlight warms air unevenly. Warm air floats up. Cooler air flows in to take the warm air's place. This motion makes wind.

9

Hot air balloons rise the way
warm air rises to create wind.
A burner powered by gas heats
the air in the balloon.
The hot air lifts the balloon.

Wind moves, but wind can
also move other things.
Wind makes flags flap.
Wind blows sand
into high dunes.

Water

Water moves in many ways.

Rain pours down from the sky.

Streams rush over waterfalls.

Drops can drip, drip, drip

from your faucet.

Electricity

Electricity gives lots of things the power to move.
Escalators are moving stairs powered by an electric motor.

Bumper cars run on electricity.
They have a long metal pole
that touches the ride's roof.
Electricity travels from the roof
to the motor to power the car.

Make a Pinwheel

What You Need

- ruler
- scissors
- paper
- pushpin
- pencil with eraser at end

1 Cut a 6-inch (15-centimeter) square out of a piece of paper.

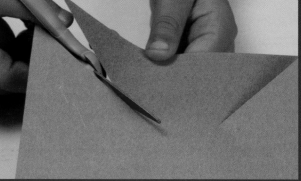

2 Cut diagonally from each corner toward the middle of the square, about halfway to the middle.

3 Fold the left corner of each side of the square toward the middle and hold.

4 Have an adult help you pin the corners in the middle with the pushpin.

5 Also have an adult push the pin into the pencil's eraser.

6 Your pinwheel is finished! Now you can take it outside or blow on it to see wind in motion.

Glossary

burner—a device with a flame to heat the air in a hot air balloon

dune—a sand hill made by wind

electricity—a form of energy caused by the movement of very tiny particles

motor—a machine that provides the power to make something run or work

Read More

Boothroyd, Jennifer. *Forces.* Lightning Bolt Books. First Physics. Minneapolis: Lerner Publications, 2011.

Stewart, Melissa. *Energy in Motion.* Rookie Read-About Science. New York: Children's Press, 2006.

Twist, Clint. *Forces & Motion.* Science Everywhere! Mankato, Minn.: NewForest Press, 2011.

Internet Sites

FactHound offers a safe, fun way to find Internet sites related to this book. All of the sites on FactHound have been researched by our staff.

Here's all you do:

Visit *www.facthound.com*

Type in this code: 9781429666077

Super-cool stuff! Check out projects, games and lots more at **www.capstonekids.com**

Index

Word Count: 192
Grade: 1
Early-Intervention Level: 21